TURNING STONES INTO Gems

THIRD EDITION

AN INSPIRATIONAL SELF-DEVELOPMENT SYSTEM

Learn how to find direction in your life and career

Sara Freeman Smith

U R Gems™ GROUP

Copyright © 1997, 1998, 2023 by Sara Freeman Smith
First Printing 1997
Second Printing 1998, Revised
Third Printing, 2023 Revised

Library of Congress Card Catalog Number: 2022921224
Names: Freeman-Smith, Sara, Author
Title: Turning Stones Into Gems

ISBN: 978-0-9662328-0-6 (paperback)

All rights reserved. No part of this publication may be reproduced, stored in a retrieval system or transmitted in any form by any means, otherwise, without the prior written permission of the publisher or author.

Edited by: M. E. Smith and Rae Bittle, WaterMark Studio & Publishing -USA, Global

Printed in the United States of America by U R Gems Group, Inc. Houston, Texas

All Scripture quotations, unless otherwise indicated, are taken from the Holy Bible, New International Version®, NIV®. Copyright ©1973, 1978, 1984, 2011 by Biblica, Inc.® Used by permission of Zondervan. All rights reserved worldwide. www.zondervan.com The "NIV" and "New International Version" are trademarks registered in the United States Patent and Trademark Office by Biblica, Inc.®

Cover and Interior Design by Black Women Publish, LLC.
Photographer, ETM Photography, Houston, Texas

Dedication

To my husband, Mack, for your love, encouragement and being there through some major storms.

To my son, Rashod, you are a gem, my precious gem!

To my adoptive parents, the late Frank and Mercury Freeman, for their unconditional love, faith, and belief in me.

To the late Erma Jean Taylor, my mother, for your love of family, and friends and the generosity that she passed on to me.

> "The best way out is always through!"
> Robert Frost

PREFACE

Turning Stones Into Gems is a personal testimony of learning how to find direction in my life and career, through a self-development process. This self-fulfillment process begins and ends with you. It starts from the inside out. I learned after nearly forty years that the void I felt in my life was due to an unfulfilled spiritual need in my career. I had to take a "running leap of faith" from the corporate world before I could see what I was missing. I did not realize how much my career directly affected my family, spiritual, and social life. Once I got off the merry-go-round of the workplace, God could get my full attention to tell me what was missing. He could tell me how I could fill the void. We spend so much of our time working or trying to find work, that very little time is left for the "real" treasures in our lives.

I looked like a gem but felt like a stone. I didn't know my true value was on the inside. I worked hard all my life at looking good on the outside; but the inside was empty. By sharing my story and self-development process with you, maybe I can make a difference in one life by turning a stone into a gem! That's how I measure my success every day of my life by touching, helping, or meaning something to someone.

Booker T. Washington once said on the meaning of success,

"I have learned that success is to be measured not so much by the position that one has reached in life but by the obstacles which one has overcome while trying to succeed."

Countless times during my childhood I was told by some friends, relatives, and society, that I was a stone and would remain a stone! Other's opinions about me one day could have become my destiny, if I allowed it. Throughout our lives, God has a way of turning your weaknesses into strengths, your pain into a gain, your impossibilities into realities, if you let Him. Let me share portions of my life that appeared to be outwardly impossibilities or stones and became awesome realities or gems!

FOREWORD

Turning Stones Into Gems is a wonderful inspirational tool that will help individuals become what God means for them to be. I highly recommend this book to anyone who is searching for direction and purpose in life. It has been a valuable resource for me and an excellent addition to my library. I would like to thank Sara for obeying God as He directed her to write this book. Many will be blessed through this work.

Rev. Walter K. Berry, Sr. Berry, Sr., Pastor
McGee Chapel Missionary Baptist Church
Houston, Texas

Acknowledgments

I am truly blessed! I thank you Lord for the ability to use my talents to benefit others in your Kingdom. I give You all the glory, love, and praise!

Thank you, Mack, for never giving up on me, although you thought I never listened... I did!

Thank you, Rashod, for your patience when Mom had "other book related" things to do. Thank you for just being you. Thank you, God, for blessing us with Rashod.

I'm grateful for my family, especially my late maternal grandmother, Alma Ray, for sharing some special moments in my life.

I'm thankful for the support of my "second" mother, the late Willie Mae Pendleton. She fulfilled the role of my mother, even though she was my mother-in-law. The best PR agent ever!

I'm especially thankful for the support and love from my late Daddy Walker, Artis Walker, Sr. Thanks to my brothers and sisters, Larkin & Regina and my late siblings; Brenda, Carol, Mary Ann, Janice, and "Spud (Artis Jr)" for loving me and allowing me to be "just me."

To all of my combined family members and friends, thank you for loving and accepting me as I am.

A very special thanks to some special friends, Rae Bittle, ConSandra Jones Harris and the late Janice Gibson. Thank you for the prayers, push, and then for helping hold the net! I could not have written this book without you and your prayers.

A big thank you Rev. Marlon D. F. Washington, "Poppa," for your "timely" visit, advice, and helping hands.

Contents

Chapter 1. My Beginning	11
Chapter 2. Your Beginning	19
Chapter 3. Am I Really Worth Anything?	23
Chapter 4. What Tools Do I Need?	27

The Six P Process

Chapter 5. Prayer	29
Chapter 6. Planning	37
Chapter 7. Passion	45
Chapter 8. Patience	47
Chapter 9. Persistence	49
Chapter 10. Pull Someone Else Up Along the Way	51

Conclusion	53
My Action Planner	57
Gratitude Prayer/Journal	65
Suggested Reading	107
About the Author	109
Other Books by the Author	111
Testimonials	113

*"The successful person is
always a learner."*
Norman V. Peale

Chapter 1
My Beginning

I entered this world on a hot and humid August day in 1954. I was born in Houston, Texas in the charity hospital. My mother, Erma Jean, was a 21-year-old, unwed Black mother with a 3-year-old son when I was born. She lived in the inner city, Fifth Ward, not a rich neighborhood but certainly not the poorest either. My mother ultimately had eight children, two boys and six girls. Five men fathered those eight children. Erma Jean married only one of them, the father of my youngest three sisters. For three of those five men, I use the term father loosely; only to imply that they impregnated my mother. A father means more than getting someone pregnant. It means taking on and fulfilling a responsibility in your child's life. My biological father, along with the two others were absent and unknown during our childhood. By society's standards, I would be considered "just another statistic" for failure, another stone in a big pile of rocks!

But God had a plan for my life; long before I was even aware there was a plan. He put the plan in motion the day I was born by giving me not one, not two but three guardian angels to care for me.

The first guardian angel was Artis Walker, Sr., the first father I knew. He met my mother while she was pregnant with me and no longer with my biological father. Daddy Walker loved my mother very much to accept her with a ready-made family of two during difficult times in the 50's. He loved and cared for me from the day I was born, as though I were his "real" daughter. I didn't know he was not my biological father until I was in grade school. Though he never married my mother, he filled the shoes of father and husband as best he knew how.

It was extremely painful learning the truth about my father from someone other than my mother. Later in my life, I had to forgive my mother for the pain I carried, because she never told me directly until I asked her.

He fathered two children with Erma Jean, a girl and boy, and remained with us for the first six years of my life. Daddy Walker accepted the role as my first father when he became my first impossibility that turned into a reality! God Blessed me with Daddy Walker to care for me when I needed him the most.

The second and third guardian angels in my life came shortly after I was born. They were my godparents, Frank and Mercury Freeman. All that I am and will ever be, I owe to them. They made the difference in my life! When I look back at my life, I was destined to be a part of their lives. They were to be a part of my life. Sometimes you think God has abandoned you, but He's always working "behind the scenes" in your life. I felt like that many times, but I didn't know God was still working His plan for me. Our age differences spanned fifty-six years and fifty-two years, that's quite a generation gap! We overcame this obstacle. They wanted a life better for me than what society had destined for me. They wanted to provide things for me that my mother could not afford. Unfortunately, they never had any children of their own but helped to raise many children of relatives during their long marriage. They were always willing to lend a helping hand.

Erma Jean moved the family to Los Angeles in the late 50's, because she wanted to provide a better opportunity for her children. Being a preschooler, I remained for six months with my godparents until she got settled with the family and Daddy Walker saved some money working in Houston. However, Los Angeles was not the land of milk and honey that my mother originally envisioned.

Nevertheless, once Erma Jean decided on anything, she was not turning back. She would do anything to make ends meet.

Both of them worked several jobs each trying to feed, clothe and shelter a family of five children. All the pressures took their toll on the relationship and Daddy Walker decided it was best for him to leave the family after nearly six years. My mother was very bright, generous, talented, and most importantly, a survivor. She would never give up on her children! I'm grateful for the time we spent together during those early years before Daddy Walker left the family. He might have left us physically but never in spirit. He tried to provide for us whenever he could with whatever he had to offer.

Once Daddy Walker left, it was never the same and I wanted to have that closeness of a complete family. I always missed being with my godparents. I enjoyed the privileges of being treated like an only child. I would constantly write to my godparents asking them to come get me and let me stay with them. They did not want to go against the wishes of my mother nor did they want to experience the heartache of when I would have to leave. But I was a very determined child. Through persistence, I convinced my mother to let me spend the summer of '62 with my godparents in Houston.

My godfather traveled by himself to pick me up for that summer. Once the train left the railroad station in Los Angeles, I said I would never go back to stay with them and I never did. I loved my Mother and siblings but always felt out of place.

When I was twelve years old, my godparents asked my mother if they could adopt and legally provide for me. By this time, my mother had married and had my three younger sisters. It was now a family of seven children and very difficult, but she didn't want to relinquish her parental rights. My godparents explained it would not mean giving up her rights as my mother, because I always knew what role she played in my life. She refused. I wanted to legally be a part of my godparent's family, because I felt like that's where I belonged.

We prayed as a family and went to see an attorney. The lawyer said it looked bad because of their age and without my mother's consent, the adoption process would be next to impossible. We went to court and met with a family law judge . I remember this moment so vividly. If only I knew that the hand of God was already working in my life. The judge asked to speak with me privately in his chambers with his law clerk present.

I sat on the side of his huge mahogany desk with my feet swinging in the chair. He asked me why I wanted to be adopted. I explained in my own words what they meant to me and my life. He turned to his law clerk and made a statement that in all his years on the bench, he was going to make a decision based on his "gut feeling" rather than facts and logic. In other words, go with his heart and not his head. He hoped he wouldn't have to regret his ruling in our favor. He granted a sixty eight year old retired man and sixty four-year-old woman parental rights of a twelve-year-old girl! That impossibility turned into my reality! From that moment forward I knew I was blessed!

The Lord blessed them with good health throughout my growing years and into college. I was blessed to graduate co-valedictorian from high school. I was awarded several major scholarships, including a full tuition Trustee Scholarship by the University of Southern California! My father only paid $50.00 for my dorm room deposit. That's all! That's God's hand at work behind the scenes.

I applied to U.S.C. in the late winter after most of the scholarships had been awarded. My S.A.T. score was less than 1,000 and I did all the paperwork on my own! Four years later, I graduated with honors with a degree in Journalism - Broadcast Management.

This stone had turned into a gem. One more impossibility turned into a reality!

I came back home after graduation due to my father's illness. My plans were to attend graduate school in business after receiving a full scholarship. I postponed my plans after my father's death several months after graduation. My mother was totally dependent on my father. She relied on him for everything—driving, budgeting & paying bills. Now, she needed to depend on me. I could get an education later, but I couldn't get another mother. The choice was easy for me.

She lived seven years after my father's death and died in October 1983 at eighty years old. Erma Jean died in March 1983, two weeks after her fiftieth birthday. Over the years, Erma Jean and I developed a stronger relationship. Her death devastated me because I always counted on her being there for me after Mom died. Major life lesson —never take anything for granted! Fortunately, both shared in the celebration of my marriage in 1981, my greatest blessing. My biggest regret was neither one got the chance to see their grandson, Rashod, my greatest joy, born in 1987. Yet, somehow I know their Spirit is watching him!

I've spent nearly twenty years working in Corporate America in various management positions. By all appearances, I would be considered successful but I didn't feel like a success on the inside. The moment I made the decision to take a leap of faith, my life changed. The focus of my message and mission became clearer since my leap. I took a running leap because if I walked out on faith, I would try to feel my way along the path. I didn't question the Lord about where I was going. I simply got out of the driver's seat and let God take over. Now the view from my backseat is fabulous!

I've decided life is like a movie. God has roles for each of us to play. Some have major roles while others have only minor parts. Yet all are important. He prepares us for our roles through life experiences. Unfortunately, we want to fast forward to the end of the movie to see the outcome. If we like it, we want the part. If we don't, we want to complain or change the roles we've been given. God is not going to clue us in on all of His plans. He wants us to trust and depend on Him and not ourselves. We can't see the value each role plays within a person's life. In God's eyes, we all serve a distinct and valuable purpose in the world. We want to ad lib our parts or make it up as we go through life. There's no need to ad lib when He has given us a great script (His Word) to study.

The character names and places may change, but the words and messages are still the same. They'll remain the same today, yesterday, tomorrow, and throughout eternity.

Studying His word will require you to give one of your most valuable assets—your time. We don't have time to study His word. Everyone is in a hurry to get somewhere. Until you get your priorities and commitments in order, you'll never have enough time. You've got to make the time and take the time today! You must practice and apply what you study; after all, everyone will be required to take tests. God's tests are a preparation for something far greater than you can imagine. You will either pass or fail, as one minister once said, "God does not grade on a curve system!" If you do not pass the test, you will repeat the class until you do.

Ever wonder why certain situations keep happening in your life? Maybe you did not learn the complete lesson from your test. When was the last time you studied for a major exam, but never tried to answer or practice solving the problems in the back of the chapter before going to the next chapter? That would be a waste of your time! If you do not apply what you learn, the knowledge you gain will be useless.

God wants us to use what we study and learn in the Bible in our lives daily. Once you pass your test, it reveals what you really believe and know in your heart. Guess what? Once you pass, you get promoted to the next level!

If life is like a movie, then mine has been similar to my favorite movie, The Wizard of Oz. I was like Dorothy, trying to find my way back home. At first, I did not encounter friends in need along my journey; instead I was the one in need. I was the one with all the empty voids. I needed to apply my brains like the Scarecrow, but with more wisdom added to my knowledge. I had used my brains for material gains most of my life. I needed courage like the Lion to take the leap of faith to do God's will. I needed a heart like the Tin Man to have compassion for the others just like me. I already had the "real godparents" and they instilled in me where I could go and get all my answers. The answers were not found in the Emerald City! I called on my Heavenly Father or the Wizard and he answered my prayer. I discovered all my answers were right inside me. My yellow brick road was already paved by God, all I needed to do was just follow it. Now, I want to share them with you. You don't need to click your heels to turn your dreams into realities!

It's not an accident that you are reading this book right now in your life. Everything happens for a reason. You have been searching for answers. You are probably feeling overwhelmed by it all. Uncertainty, frustration, and incompleteness are just a few of your feelings. God has directed you to this book as a starting point on your journey to help you find your answers. Somewhere within these pages, there's a message just for you. Just begin to pay attention.

Remember when you were in grade school, you would connect the alphabets or numbers in proper order to make a picture. Unless you linked together each letter or number, you could not see the big picture. If you skipped a letter or number, it would distort the picture. Pay attention and begin to connect the dots in your life and circumstances! *Turning Stones Into Gems* is the tool you need to help you make the connections in your life and career!

Now turn the page to begin your successful journey on turning stones into gems!

> *"A passion to do whatever you do in a passionate way. Then you do it well."*
> Oscar de la Renta

Chapter 2
Your Beginning

Are you a precious gem or a worthless stone? Do you feel like you are surrounded by other precious and valuable gems or stuck in the middle of a rock pile with the useless rocks and stones? Do you wonder why You had to be a worthless stone while others are valuable gems? If you are a precious gem surrounded by other valuable gems, you are truly Blessed! Keep reading this book to polish your tools needed to maintain your true value.

On the other hand, you are doubly Blessed if you are a stone. You're as valuable as the gem, because the stone and gem are the same. The only difference is what you see on the outside instead of knowing that the real value is on the inside of the stone. You're blessed because you recognize where you are in, a Rock—in—a—Pile. Some people don't even realize they're in a rock pile, living between other rocks and stones . It's a blessing to know where you are before you can know where you want to go.

But more importantly, you're already Blessed with the ability to come out of the Rock-in-a-pile to become a gem! God gave us all unique and different talents, gifts, and abilities. Each of us has valuable resources and potential locked deep inside of us. Some "stones" need a helping hand to unlock their hidden potential in life. It all begins on the inside.

Chapter 2. Your Beginning

This book will begin to help you find out how to get the key to "unlock" your maximum potential. You must first understand that you possess unlimited power to achieve any goal you want. You have immense value and resources stored inside you, despite the number of failures, obstacles, shortcomings, or personal and professional difficulties you may have experienced. You're a Gem!

> ***Begin to see it, believe it,***
> ***and you'll become it!***

Acres of Diamonds

This is a story of a poor African who struggled for years to earn a living as a farmer. His soil was rocky, which made it difficult to cultivate his crops. The farmer became very disillusioned with his future and decided to pursue his dream to become wealthy by following other men who had sought and found their fame and fortune. They had discovered diamonds in his homeland After hastily selling his farm, the farmer spent his remaining years searching for diamonds throughout Africa. But he never discovered a diamond. Finally, after the farmer realized he was broke and would never fulfill his dream, he took his life.

One day the second farmer who had purchased the farm discovered a large and unusual stone in his field. He found out it was an extremely valuable diamond the second farmer later learned his property was covered with acres and acres of diamonds. His land later became known as one of the richest diamond mines in the world!

If only the first farmer knew that he owned "acres and acres of diamonds" all the time . A lot of us are much like the first farmer, forever searching for "acres of diamonds" in our lifetime. We may leave our homes, our jobs, our families, our friends, our churches, and even our God to look for them. If only we knew, the real treasures are right in front of us, ourselves!

It seems that many people are searching for true meaning, purpose, and value in their lives today. Everything in our world has a value attached to it. Some things in life have greater value than others.

A value means to rate someone or something in usefulness, importance, or general worth. We are all precious gems in God's sight. We are more precious than silver or gold to our Father. I know we all have "value" in God's kingdom. God does not make mistakes or junk! No one can place a price tag on our "true divine worth" in His kingdom.

> *"No one can put you down without your permission."*
> Anna Eleanor Roosevelt

Chapter 3
Am I Really Worth Anything?

First common mistake, we try to determine our value based on our circumstances or our surroundings, just like the first farmer did in the story. Do not let your circumstances, your surroundings, or negative individuals determine your destiny or worth in life.

Some of us begin a seemingly never ending search for something of value in our lives. Some of us are more willing to work harder at trying to find it than others. Yet, what we are seeking to discover really is not that hard to find, once you know where to look and what you are looking for. The second farmer knew to look in his *own backyard* and then realized that the stones could have value, if he looked deep inside of them.

It was not an easy task to crack open the stone. It took a lot of hard work and special tools to carve, chisel, and cut away all of the "old worthless debris" from the outer shell of the rock. The second farmer knew he had to take this unusual stone to a gem specialist to determine its value. The Specialist in our life is God. The gem specialist was knowledgeable in every aspect of that gem. He had the "proper tools" necessary to begin the process of "turning stones into gems." God has given us the tools. We just need to ask our Specialist how to use them.

God has given us the tools to be used diligently to get to the "real gems" in our lives. It will be very hard work shedding and leaving all of our old baggage or outer debris from the rock. Success only comes before the word work in the dictionary, everywhere else, you must work hard to achieve success.

Did you realize that all of your past failures, misfortunes, obstacles, trials, hardships, failed relationships, chemical and alcohol addictions, imprisonments, physical or mental disabilities, and any other "challenging" experiences gave you the tools you needed to be successful? Always remember what a stone looks like before it becomes a gem. If you look at your life from the outside or from the surface, you'll see all of the outer, crusty debris that took years to cover up the real beauty of the gem, which is on the inside of the stone. The "difficult" times in our lives are like the outer surface of a stone. If it took years to accumulate the "debris" in our lives, it stands to reason, it would take time for us to get to the core of our real beauty or value.

Just like our gems specialist, special tools are required to cut and carve away the unwanted "debris" of our life. Remember, once you carve away the debris, throw it away, get rid of it! Too often we hold on to the waste instead of just letting it go. Forget the past and leave it in the past! If you continue to hold on to the debris it will weigh you down. Anything that adds weight, will slow you or stop you from reaching your goal.

The debris in your life can include negative people or other "stones" in the rock pile. These are the toxic people who tear you down instead of trying to build you up! Why do you need someone for that when you have been doing a convincing job by yourself for all these years. If someone cannot build you up, you don't need their help to tear yourself down. Get rid of the negative people or stones in your life. Once you decide to come out of the rock pile and become a gem, leave the other rocks in the pile that do not believe in you or in themselves. The old saying, " misery loves company" is true. They want you to remain in the rock pile with them, because they do not realize they are gems also. You cannot help anyone unless they want to help themselves. Abraham Lincoln said, "You cannot help men and women permanently by doing for them, what they could and should do for themselves." They will still be in the rock pile years from now, wondering how you got out and they did not.

You have taken the most important step. You've come out of the rock pile! A gem should be among other "gems" to appreciate its beauty and value. When you want to find a precious gem, you don't look for one in a rock pile, you go to a fine jewelry store or department store with the other precious jewels. If you stay in the rock pile, you will begin to walk like a rock, talk like a rock, think like a rock and look like a rock.

Finally, you will notice that people will treat you like a rock, because you are not letting your true beauty and value glow.

Determine who are the "stones" in your life and let them go! Walk away, give them away, have a Midnight Madness clearance sale of all the negative people in your life! BOGO-Buy one negative person, get one free! You will feel better and notice an immediate difference in your life.

> *"If you can't change your fate, change your attitude!"*
> **Amy Tan**

Chapter 4
What Tools Do I Need?

Did you realize that you already have the necessary tools to begin the process? Probably not, and if you do, you may not know how to use them. Our Specialist gave each of us the tools we need to develop our inner value. This is the most difficult step of all, because it requires long, hard, and tedious work just like the second farmer was willing to do. The process of turning a stone into a gem will take time. One of our most valuable assets is our time. Time waits for no one. It cannot be recovered and we can never get enough of it. The time needed to develop will be different for each individual. Do not compare what it takes for someone else to develop into the gem with what it will take for you.

The tools that you will need to begin the process of development from a stone into a gem are called the:

Six P System™
- Prayer
- Planning
- Passion
- Patience
- Persistence
- Pull Someone Else Along the Way

*God can't fix it
until you face it!*

Chapter 5
Prayer: Conversations with God

All your plans should begin and end in prayer. Offer all your plans to God before you begin to plan anything. The power of prayer is the way we communicate to God. We talk with God through our prayers. Just imagine, you need help and you only have a phone. Why wouldn't you use the phone to call for help? A call for help could be to the police, ambulance, or fire department; depending on your particular situation. Once the phone call has been placed, you feel a little less anxious or nervous. Some of our original fears seem to diminish, because you know if you just wait awhile you'll hear a siren or see the flashing lights getting closer.

Well, our Father is just a prayer away. When you need help, you hit a button on the cell or dial 9-1-1, request help and wait because you know help is on its way! Prayer can be your call to 9-1-1. Place your request for help and just wait on God to send an answer to your request. Through prayer, you will develop a stronger faith and trust in God, because you have to wait for an answer or help to arrive.

Prayer = Planning

Notice I said to *request* help with your plan. Do not tell God what you plan to do! Too often we tell God how to do His business, especially when it relates to us. After all, we think who better knows what's good for us than ourselves! Well, that's like telling God what you want Him to do and how He ought to do it! So why do you need Him? Just do it yourself!

Would you even consider calling 9-1-1 for help and proceeding to tell the operator what to do? Would you tell the fire or police department how to put a chemical fire out or disarm criminals? Absolutely not! You put your trust and faith in the hands of the experts to make the right decisions for your safety and well-being.

Yet, we want God to okay our plans before we ask if they're the right plans for our life. Is there something wrong with this picture? Don't be confused and ask for your answers. Instead, always pray for your **requests.** *Pray first and plan afterwards.*

> *"Trust in the Lord with all your heart and lean not on your own understanding; in all your ways acknowledge Him, and he will make your paths straight."*
> *Proverbs 3:5-6*

Prayer = Vision

Once you begin to trust in the Lord, your plans will begin to fall into place. Too often, we try to figure out God's business. No one can figure out what God's plan is for you except God, so stop trying. Let go and let God! I tried for years to figure out how to plan my life and never got a clear picture. My prayer was my will to be done in my life! I wanted to do things that would benefit me, not God. In this life, it's not about you or me. It's all about God and His Glory. Once I prayed for His will in my life and all my plans, He began to make my vision clear. God will give you the vision and He will make the provisions too! You must get out of God's business, let God take over and just do! Through prayer, you'll begin to see yourself accomplishing what God has told you to do.

Prayer = Self-Esteem

Prayer is the key that unlocks the door to faith. Once you have faith in God, you get a stronger belief in yourself. If you do not believe in yourself, all your plans will be useless. If you do not believe that you are a valuable gem, you certainly cannot convince others to believe in you. If you do not allow your beauty to shine, how can anyone else see it?

Begin to see it, believe it and you'll become it! You must choose to either live up to your expectations or down to others expectations of you. Remember, you are never alone. He will always be there even when you think He's not.

Remember, the *stones* in your life will try to convince you that everything you try will fail. If you allow the *stones* to lower your self-esteem, you will never achieve your goals. Start today to apply the **B.U.L.I.**™ (pronounced bully) process to improve your self-development. Believe, understand, love and invest in yourself in every endeavor!

> *"I can do everything through Him who gives me strength."*
> *Philippians 4:13*

Believe in Yourself

Understand Yourself

Love Yourself

Invest in Yourself

Know that you are a valuable gem and worthy of respect!

Believe in Yourself

Visualize yourself accomplishing whatever goals you want to achieve. You must believe in yourself before others will believe in you. You must have faith and trust in God and yourself.

"What I have said, that will I bring about, what I have planned, that I will do." Isaiah 46:11

Understand Yourself

Know who you are, what you are capable of doing, and know your strengths and weaknesses. Understand that God made us all gems, yet no one is perfect! Ask God for understanding and know He will answer. The "real you" will be revealed.

"... that He understands, and knows me." Jeremiah 9:24

Love Yourself

See your own unique qualities over others. Stop comparing yourself to someone else. Work on strengthening your best qualities. Improve or let go of those qualities you like the least. Think about who you really want to be and be thankful for you! Do not change because others want you to change. Change your life because you feel the need to change!

Invest in Yourself

You must make deposits in yourself! Take time out to develop and improve you! If you don't take care of yourself mentally, physically, and emotionally, how can you take care of anyone else? We are accustomed to giving too much of ourselves - major withdrawals.

We forget to replenish ourselves—make deposits. In order for any investment to grow in value, you must put something into it! You must apply the B.U.L.I.™ process daily in your life to be effective. Others will begin to see the true gem God has purposed and called you to be. God has declared you victorious!

"And those he predestined, he also called; those he called, he also justified; those he justified, he also glorified . . . if God is for us who can be against us?" Romans 8:30-31

Prayer = Positive Attitude

Prayer will give you a positive attitude about your work, situations, plans, etc. Remember, once you get rid of the negative people in your life, surround yourself with positive people and thoughts. You're no longer a Rock-in-a-Pile! Once you're out of the rock pile, you can view the world from a positive perspective. Do not dwell on what you lack, but become grateful for the things you have in your life. Develop an **attitude of gratitude** about your daily life. You can begin to search for the positives, the little things that you already have in your possession. In these days, it's not difficult to be inundated with tons of negative comments, behavior, situations and people through social media, news, co-workers family and friends

An attitude is the way you think on the inside that shows up on the outside. Attitude shows up in your behavior. It is important that you get a good dose of positive affirmations every day to overcome the negative influences we face every day. Prayer is your first source.

Secondly, begin to keep a Prayer/Gratitude journal like the one recommended under Suggested Reading in the back of this book or just a plain notebook. Each day think and write down at least three things, persons, places or whatever you are thankful for having in your life. When you write it down, you own it! When you own something, you treasure it, value it, nurture it, and develop it. Once you begin to dwell on the things you have, the more you will get out of what you have.

Attitudes are like the flu and can be extremely contagious! Be sure yours is worth catching daily if others come in contact with you!

Write down several positive and inspiring statements that will make you feel good about yourself and what you do daily. Make at least five copies of the statements and put them where you will see them constantly. Repeat these statements to yourself at least ten times every day for at least six to eight weeks. Here's a sample of what I say (with feeling) to myself daily:

Thank you God for providing my daily bread. I'm an incredible being with unlimited potential. I'm too blessed to be stressed! I'm a winner!

I taped this statement on my bathroom mirror, on my computer, inside my daily planner, inside my car, and inside my portfolio or briefcase. It starts my day on a positive note, no matter what happens. You must empty your mind of negative thoughts daily! Replace them with positive thoughts and images of yourself achieving your goals.

Prayer = Intercession

Don't forget to ask others to pray for you and your plans too! The power of intercessory prayer is awesome and it works! Try Him! Don't take my word, read a book called, "*What Happens When Women Pray*" by Evelyn Christenson. Through many personal documented accounts from across the country, the power of intercessory prayer is phenomenal! Ask Him for a prayer partner or prayer group to join or form, then wait for His answer. Just as others pray for you, always think of others in need of prayer. Don't just pray for immediate family and friends, pray for your job, co-workers, supervisors, pastor, church leaders and members and even your enemies. Ask Him for the words. He knows every need!

Here are some daily prayers that will fill your life with peace, joy, and power to overcome any challenge you may face. Pray with passion and total faith in God. Expect an answer!

Our Father in Heaven, it is by Your Grace that I have the many abilities/talents that make me helpful to others and to Your church. By Your Grace, may I have the willingness to sacrifice my selfish interests and to use Your gifts for You and Your people. Lord, help me to perceive the talent you have given me and guide me in putting them to work for Your glory and edification. I acknowledge You in all that I do and I give to You all my praise, love and thanks! In Jesus' name, I pray, AMEN!

My Daily Prayer*
Our Father, I don't know what my day holds. I don't know what's in it for You and me but I'm all Yours, I'm your willing vessel. You're my Potter and I'm Your clay. Today belongs to You, not me. Please Lord, I want You to guide me, one step at a time, not my words but Your words, not my thoughts but Your thoughts, not my way but Your way.

I want the Holy Spirit to mark my every step. Please stop me if I'm moving in the wrong direction or with the wrong people. Push me if I'm slow and lazy. Shake me back to my senses if I get out of line, but don't let me go my own way. Fill me Lord today with Your Peace, Your Joy and Your Power. Help me to use the talents and gifts you've given me to glorify and edify Your name.

Let me make a difference in someone's life today. I love you Lord, I praise you, I thank you in all my ways. Lord, fill me and use me in Jesus' name, I pray, AMEN!

Chapter 6
Planning: Road Map for Success

How will you become the type of gem you want to be without a plan or map to follow? A gem specialist knows exactly how to bring out the best luster and beauty of each gem through the shaping and refining of the stone. Each gem can be sized and shaped differently, but all will ultimately achieve crowning glory through the refining process. Some gems maintain their beauty in a variety of shapes such as oval, diamond, round, marquise, and many other forms.

Our Specialist has given each of us different kinds of talent and gifts that should be used to fulfill our purpose and His will in our life. It may seem that some people have more gifts and talents than others, but we cannot measure the magnitude of gifts, only God can do that. All our gifts can be used to serve the church and God. He wants to melt, mold, and shape us into the best form possible to serve Him. Would you dare tell the gem specialist how to cut and shape a diamond in the rough? No, you would ask him for his professional advice and expect him to give you his answer. Would you then tell God what's best for you in your career?

You must ask Him to reveal His plan to you, step by step. Trust in Him to bring out all of your inner talents and gifts, some of which you may not realize you already have. You may not understand why, but you will ultimately become the finished product - a true Gem!

What an awesome promise from God for you and His plan for your life and career! Our Father already has a plan for you. It's up to you to ask His plan and more important, be willing to follow it to bring out your best qualities. Can you follow His instructions? He will give you free will to choose your plan or His plan. The choice is yours. However, remember with every choice you make you will have a consequence. If you follow His plan, you know the benefits He will give you from His Word. Can you say the same about your plan?

> *"For I know the plans I have for you," declares the Lord, "plans to prosper you and not to harm you, plans to give you hope and a future. Then you will call upon me and come and pray to me, and I will listen to you. You will seek me and find me when you seek me with all your heart. I will be found by you."*
> **Jeremiah 29:11-14**

But often, your plans fail because you failed to plan. Can you imagine going on a long summer driving vacation to the Grand Canyon without a map? ? Would you want to take that trip? Often we know where we want to go, but just do not know the best way to get there. It has been said, success is a journey not a destination. To have a successful journey, you need a map to get there!

First, ask yourself certain questions before beginning your journey.

- Do I want to achieve this journey very fast?
- Do I want to take my time and sight see along the way?
- Do I need to know everything about the Grand Canyon before I get there?
- What will I do when I get there?
- Where will I stay? How long will I stay?
- What will I do if something happens along the way?

- Do I have enough money? Any extra?
- Do I go alone, with friends, family, or a tour group?
- Why did I pick the Grand Canyon?
- What do I hope to learn from the trip?

These same questions can apply to your career and life, only the subject would change. It can be difficult trying to find direction for your life without ever asking Him. Yet, that's what a lot of us do. **Ask God, what is Your will and He will answer!**

When I was growing up, everyone selected a career based on how much money you could earn; or if it was a stable profession; or if it was a family profession. No one thought about using the talents and gifts God gave us to fulfill His will. Eventually, your life revolved around your career. You chose your career based on circumstances and other people. Begin to think back while growing up, what did you dream about doing? Did you think it was just a dream? Or did someone discourage you from pursuing your dream? You really wanted to do one thing, but you listened to society and other people's opinion because your dreams appeared impossible for you to achieve. Accepting society's destiny for your life was easier than believing in yourself and God's plan.

> *"In his heart a man plans his course, but the Lord determines his steps."*
> **Proverbs 16:9**

Ask yourself, am I happy with my life or career choice? If not, begin to ask God about His plans for your career; especially if your choices have not been working lately, why not try His plans! You must be willing to ask Him. *Ask Him this question, what is Your will?* Determine what your talents and gifts are and begin to apply them to your career or life.

Ask Yourself These Questions . . .
Write your answers down.
(Complete your Action Planner in the back)

- Do I want to achieve this career endeavor in the shortest time possible? Why?
- Do I want to take my time and go step by step into this career? Why?
- How much education or training will I need?
- Do I have the skills to be successful?
- What skills do I need to be successful
- How do I define success? Is it Cars, money, job, title, house, influential people?
- Why don't I feel good about what I do?
- What would I do if I didn't have to work?
- In my spare time, what do I really enjoy doing?
- Do I have what it takes to become a business owner?
- What would I do if I fail?
- Would I be willing to start over again? Why not?
- Can I afford not to try?
- What am I really good at doing?
- Now that I have all these answers, where do I go from here?

Don't stop there!

Start a list of people to contact for information. List places to contact to begin your research. The results will be amazing when you ask for help. It's not what you ask but how you ask it, that's important. Always keep an attitude of gratitude and appreciation when asking for help. Remember to have a sincere desire to gain as much information as possible.

Contact/Name	Reason
1.	
2.	
3.	
4.	
5.	
6.	

Additional Space for Answers, Contacts, Follow-up Information & Notes

Discovering what you are best at doing.

The next step is to take a self-evaluation of your true career abilities, not just your interests and then match them to the right career track. I recommend a career assessment profile which measures your aptitude; what you can do now and what you can do in the future, if given the opportunity to learn. Most career assessment profiles measure your career interest inventory; what you think you might like to do and how your interests align with various careers. There is a wide range of free online career assessments available online for free and some for a cost, do your research and begin your fact finding journey!

One assessment that I have recommended and found very resourceful for years is a government sponsored one which is a good start to your journey. The *O*Net Interest Profiler* is a self-directed assessment developed by the US Department of Labor to help guide you to the best careers based on your interests and skills. This is a very comprehensive assessment that will also provide additional information for educational requirements. The US Department of Labor site is a wealth of resources regarding salaries and occupations in high demand jobs as well. This is the link to access the assessment: **http://www.mynextmove.org/explore/ip**

I really would like to be a professional singer. I have always had a strong interest in singing . However , I have one slight problem; I can't sing! I really tried but God did not bless me with the gift of song. I could really struggle on the singing circuit to make it, but I know I cannot sing. I could probably etch a meager living, but would never find true success.

You could be a frustrated accountant that could be an excellent marketing representative for a financial planning firm. You could be a mediocre engineer that could be an excellent public relations consultant. You could be working for someone else when you could be an excellent business owner.

So what's stopping you? You must understand your strengths

and your weaknesses and what you can do. Take the career assessment profile and those questions will be answered. Remember, you are never too old to change or start a career. There are numerous career assessment profiles online that you may want to consider to supplement what you learn from the O*Net profile.

Now that you have the answers, take the following steps:

1. Take a leap of faith—Walk by faith not by sight!

2. Know that God will be there with a safety net

3. Obey God and follow your plan

4. Trust God for the results

Listen to your heart and not your mind. Be prepared not to rely on family and friends, because they will probably think you're crazy and discourage you! Our ways are not God's ways. Don't over analyze or try to figure anything out. It's already been done for you!

Knowledge

The planning process should always include time for gaining knowledge along the way. Never stop learning! Always take the time to learn as much as you can about what interests you. As you acquire knowledge, pray for wisdom and discernment. Knowledge is worthless if you cannot apply it wisely. Be willing to change if needed.

"God, grant me the serenity to accept the things I cannot change, courage to change the things I can, and the wisdom to know the difference." Serenity Prayer/Alcoholics Anonymous

> *"A man's steps are directed by the Lord. How then can anyone understand his own way?"*
> **Proverbs 20:24**

Chapter 7
Passion

The first two steps are the most critical in the Six P System. You must complete them both before you can apply the other P's in the system.

You must have a strong passion about a goal or plan to remain focused. You will have natural enthusiasm or desire for what you want to do especially if you love what you do. If you have determined from the career aptitude assessments what you can do well, then get excited about it. If you want to be the best at what you do, develop a passion to excel at it. Become an expert at what you do.

Passion can mean making a strong commitment to doing the little tedious details repeatedly until you become very competent. When you become competent , that's the first step to achieving success.

When it comes to your life and career, you must know what motivates you. Ask yourself, what really motivates me? Money, cars, social status, family, job title or competitions are all common motivators. If you have passion, you will gain motivation and drive which will provide the energy to sustain you during your success journey. Without passion, whatever you do will be another chore or a job.

When you have passion, your job becomes an avocation or hobby instead of an occupation. You do it whether you're paid or not!

That's true passion.

If you do what you love, then you will do it well. If you do it well, you will be compensated accordingly. Develop a passion for anything you do and want to do it well!

***Excellence** can be attained if you...*

***Care** more than others think is wise...*

***Risk** more than others think is safe...*

***Dream** more than others think is practical...*

***Expect** more than others think is possible.*

Anonymous

Chapter 8
Patience

Experience teaches us patience. You gain experience by doing. In our society, patience is rarely practiced. Everyone's in a hurry to get somewhere or something. Our attitudes reflect our lack of patience. We want it now! We microwave our meals. We overindulge in fast foods. We watch television or social media for our news. We drive rather than walk. We fly rather than drive. We litigate rather than mediate.

If you lack the patience, it's difficult to gain complete understanding of a situation. Remember our trip to the Grand Canyon? How can you appreciate its natural beauty if you fly over it at night? The Bible says a patient man gains understanding . While you are learning to wait, you gain valuable experience!

"But they that wait upon the Lord shall renew their strength."
Isaiah 40:31

What would you do if the microwave and fast food restaurants no longer existed? You would learn to cook. You would learn by making some mistakes , but patience would allow you to endure the learning experience.

Patience allows you to remain steadfast in face of adversity, opposition, or difficulty. Gaining patience teaches you to have faith in God and not yourself. True faith pleases God. Learning patience means bearing trials without complaining. That can be very difficult without help from above. Studying God's word will give you the patience needed to overcome any anxiety. Patience will prepare you for a greater gain or reward. **Patience develops a love relationship with God!**

Learning to have patience is like baking a cake. You must mix different types of ingredients together to make the batter. God must thoroughly mix the batter or beat it to get the lumps out. Your experiences in life are the lumps in the batter. They may be painful, but necessary. God bakes the batter at a high temperature for a specified time. The oven is extremely hot! Yet the batter must remain in the oven until it's done or you could ruin the cake. You cannot lower the temperature or turn off the oven unless you want to spoil the cake. Does this sound like your experiences in your life and career? They may be difficult but they have a value or purpose. Just sweat it out in the oven for a while and learn to be patient. It's well worth the wait!

"... but to imitate those who through faith and patience inherit what has been promised." Hebrews 6:12

Chapter 9
Persistence

"Not only so, but we also rejoice in our sufferings, because we know that suffering produces perseverance, perseverance, builds character; and character springs hope. And hope does not disappoint us because God has poured out his love into our hearts by the Holy Spirit, whom he has given us." Romans 5:3-5

Persistence is never giving up or quitting. You must have the self-discipline and determination to keep trying to reach your goal in your life or career. Persistence means to do something even when you don't want to do it, because you face opposition.

See it, believe it, become it!

Never, ever give up believing in yourself. If you believe in yourself, eventually everyone else will believe in you too! Remember to practice the B.U.L.I. System™ in Chapter 5.

"Forgetting what is behind and straining toward what is ahead, I press on toward the goal to win the prize for which God has called me heavenward in Jesus Christ." Philippians 3:13-14

Persistence is critical in life when you get knocked down (we all will fall down at some point). Don't look for the person who knocked you down. It's only important that you look for a way to get up! You may have to get up repeatedly, but don't quit until you reach your goal! You will face opposition or obstacles in your life perhaps more than others. Persistence will overcome those obstacles and you will achieve ultimate success. Remember, the word success only comes before the word work in the dictionary. In life you must work hard to achieve true success!

> *"Shoot for the moon, even if you miss it, you'll land among the stars!"*
> **Les Brown**

"I've learned that success is to be measured not so much by the position that one has reached in life but by the obstacles which one has overcome while trying to succeed."
- *Booker T. Washington*

Chapter 10
Pull Someone Else Along the Way

The final step in your journey, as you achieve success, is simply to help pull someone up along the way. When you have been blessed, you should pass it on. Learn to help and give something back to others and your success will be far greater than your expectations. Success is meaningless without others to share it in your life. Be careful how you measure your success. If it's all material gain, it can be lost! If success is giving of yourself, that's what will last a lifetime!

"We make a living by what we get, we make a LIFE by what we give."
-Winston Churchill

Once you become the gem that God meant for you to be, help someone else become a gem too! Help provide a map or explain how to use the tools for someone else who is beginning their success journey. Never forget to give God the glory for your success. After all, it is by His grace that you have the many qualities, talents , and abilities that make you a precious and valuable gem in His kingdom. Acknowledge Him in all that you do. Give God the glory, praise and thanks because you are a gem!

> *"You were born to win. Start thinking, speaking, and acting like a winner."*
> *Susan L. Taylor*

Conclusion

Begin to keep an ***Attitude of Gratitude*** Prayer Journal every day. The power of a gratitude/prayer journal is awesome! Keeping a journal helps you develop daily discipline about maintaining an attitude of gratefulness. I began keeping a daily journal when I started to write this book. All of my minor and major victories, frustrations, prayer requests and daily gratitude associated with this book was recorded. I wrote *Turning Stones Into Gems* in thirty days through the power of prayer and God's grace! Yes, I wrote it in thirty days. It was self-published and sold two weeks later!

By keeping a journal, it taught me several important lessons about my journey. First, the journal improved my relationship with God. It allows you to spend more time thinking about God's goodness and grace in your life. Secondly, the journal helped me connect the dots along my journey. The journal provides spiritual landmarks where God answers your prayers even when you didn't think He was paying attention! It's written down. You can't forget what He did for you last week, last month, or last year! The picture will become clearer as you continue your journey to where God is leading you.

"Then the Lord said to Moses write this on a scroll as something to be remembered... "Exodus 17:14

Best of all, the journal reminded me to pray for others' needs. Usually, we say we will pray for one another but do we really pray? You will begin to think of other people in different circumstances and with special needs. If you write it down, you take it seriously. Intercessory prayer (praying for others) is extremely effective when it's done sincerely. It works! Intercessory prayer takes the focus off of you and focuses on others. If you pray for something, God will answer! It may not be the answer you wanted but He will answer.

> **What I Ought To Do**
>
> *I am only one, but I am one; I cannot do everything, but I can do something!*
>
> *And what I can do, I ought to do and what I ought to do,*
>
> *By the grace of God, I will do!*
>
> ***Cannon Farrar***

Start keeping your journal today! Don't worry about how much to write down, just write something down! List at least three things, events, places, people, etc. that you are thankful for. Keep this journal at least for a month and review it after a week. You will begin to notice results in your life and others.

Please start keeping a journal after reading this book even if it's a simple notebook or download one online. If you have never had a journal, read the book by Sarah Ban Breathnach, Simple Abundance Journal of Gratitude. I learned about it from Oprah Winfrey's interview with her. It was so simple and clear yet profound! I immediately started journaling and was amazed by the clarity of God's plan for me with this book. Keep your focus on the positives, what you have versus what you lack. When praises go up the blessings come down!

"The talent of success is nothing more than doing what you can do well, and doing well whatever you do! -Henry Longfellow

The most important step toward your success is the doing! You must do something! May God bless you in all your endeavors.

There are acres of gems inside each of us!

> *If you don't know where you're going, any road will take you there.*
> **Old Proverb**

My Action Planner
Career

Where do I spend most of my time?

Take a look at your priorities. Please add the hours and be honest and add up the amount of time for each.

        Amount of time   Ranking

At work or looking for work

_____   _____

Commuting to work

_____   _____

Work related functions outside the job
(Professional Organizations, Committees,
dinners Networking, etc.),

_____   _____

My Action Planner
Family/Friends

Answers based on weekly hours.

Amount of time   Ranking

Time doing chores, clean up, cooking, etc.

_____   _____

If you are married, quality time doing
 fun things with a spouse

_____   _____

If you have children, time doing
homework, talking, games, sports,
activities after school, etc.

_____   _____

If single, time doing things for
yourself or friends (not job related)

_____   _____

My Action Planner
Spiritual

Answers based on weekly hours

      Amount of time   Ranking

How often do you attend a church or religious activity?

_____   _____

Involved in church activities or functions

_____   _____

Reading or studying the Bible?

_____   _____

Praying and meditating

_____   _____

My Action Planner
Social & Community

Answers based on weekly hours.

Amount of time   Ranking

Socializing with friends and family

_____   _____

Volunteer activities in the community
and school, sports, gym, etc.

_____   _____

Traveling, shopping, etc.

_____   _____

Where do your priorities rank?

_____   _____

My Action Planner
You

Most Important

Did you fit in any time for you?

If you don't take care of yourself, how can you take care of your other priorities? Take time out or make the time for yourself and your health!

Time spent exercising, workouts,
walking, etc.

_____   _____

Time spent on self-development/improvement
(Books, tapes, seminars, classes, training, etc.)

_____   _____

Remember to take care of you, you're all you got! Don't forget, you're worth it because you are a GEM!

Are you happy with your priorities?
If your answer is no, please continue...
If your answer is yes, then skip to the Gratitude Journal
but just for fun, look anyway...

My Action Planner
Priorities

Your priorities should be:

1. Spiritual
2. You
3. Family
4. Career
5. Social/Community

If you want to restructure your priorities, begin by making a commitment to yourself and family to change. Most importantly, learn to say no! Let your family hold you accountable for commitments - no excuses.

If it is to be, it's up to me.

"You can get everything in life you want if you help enough other people get what they want."
- Zig Ziglar

My Action Planner
Priorities

Start with little projects or tasks unless you're ready to leap! Begin by giving up something... and adding more time to something else. Ask your family what they would like to do as a family. You might be amazed by their answers.

Less Of   More Of

_____   _____

_____   _____

_____   _____

You must develop an attitude of accountability. You can become more proactive about your priorities. Anticipate things can go wrong but have an alternative or back-up plan in case it's needed. You are the only one that can change you!

> *"What really matters is what happens in us and not to us."*

Gratitude/Prayer Journal

This practice teaches you to focus on what you have and you'll get more of what you have. Never concentrate on what you don't have because you'll never get enough of what you don't have!

Develop an attitude of gratitude each day!

My Personal Commitment

I promise to devote a few moments each day to think, write and meditate about the many blessings and things in life I have to be thankful.

Gratitude/Prayer Journal

Date _____

"Trust in the Lord with all your heart, lean not on your own understanding. In all your ways acknowledge Him, and He will make your paths straight." Proverbs 3:5-6

_____
_____
_____
_____
_____
_____
_____
_____
_____
_____
_____

"Do not let what you cannot do interfere with what you can do."
- John Wooden

Gratitude/Prayer Journal

Date _____

"Trust in the Lord with all your heart, lean not on your own understanding. In all your ways acknowledge Him, and He will make your paths straight." Proverbs 3:5-6

_____

_____

_____

_____

_____

_____

_____

_____

_____

_____

"Ability is what you're capable of doing. Motivation determines what you do. Attitude determines how well you do it." - Lou Holtz

Gratitude/Prayer Journal

Date _____

"Trust in the Lord with all your heart, lean not on your own understanding. In all your ways acknowledge Him, and He will make your paths straight." Proverbs 3:5-6

_____
_____
_____
_____
_____
_____
_____
_____
_____
_____
_____

"You are a Gem!" - Sara Freeman Smith

Gratitude/Prayer Journal

Date _____

"Trust in the Lord with all your heart, lean not on your own understanding. In all your ways acknowledge Him, and He will make your paths straight." Proverbs 3:5-6

_____

_____

_____

_____

_____

_____

_____

_____

_____

_____

"When you get to the end of your rope, tie a knot and hang on."
- Franklin D. Roosevelt

Notes/Meditations/Reminders

Notes/Meditations/Reminders

Gratitude/Prayer Journal

Date _____

"Ask and it will be given unto you; seek and you will find; knock and the door will be opened to you." Matthew 7:7

_____

_____

_____

_____

_____

_____

_____

_____

_____

_____

_____

_____

"Be careful for nothing, prayerful for everything, thankful for anything." - Dwight L. Moody

Gratitude/Prayer Journal

Date _____

"Ask and it will be given unto you; seek and you will find; knock and the door will be opened to you." Matthew 7:7

_____

_____

_____

_____

_____

_____

_____

_____

_____

"There will never be another me, so I'll make the most of myself."
- Robert Schuller

Gratitude/Prayer Journal

Date _____

"Ask and it will be given unto you; seek and you will find; knock and the door will be opened to you." Matthew 7:7

_____

_____

_____

_____

_____

_____

_____

_____

_____

_____

_____

"Real failure is failing to make the most of the gifts God has given you!"
- Robert Schuller

Gratitude/Prayer Journal

Date _____

"Ask and it will be given unto you; seek and you will find; knock and the door will be opened to you." Matthew 7:7

_____

_____

_____

_____

_____

_____

_____

_____

_____

_____

"You never achieve real success unless you love what you are doing."
- Dale Carnegie

Gratitude/Prayer Journal

Date _____

"Ask and it will be given unto you; seek and you will find; knock and the door will be opened to you." Matthew 7:7

_____

_____

_____

_____

_____

_____

_____

_____

_____

_____

"The only alternative to perseverance is failure."
- Anonymous

Notes/Meditations/Reminders

Gratitude/Prayer Journal

Date _____

"Commit to the Lord whatever you do and your plans will succeed." Proverbs 16:3

"Failure is only the opportunity to begin again more intelligently."
- Henry Ford

Gratitude/Prayer Journal

Date _____

"Commit to the Lord whatever you do and your plans will succeed." Proverbs 16:3

_____

_____

_____

_____

_____

_____

_____

_____

_____

_____

"We tend to get what we expect."
- Norman V. Peale

Gratitude/Prayer Journal

Date _____

"Commit to the Lord whatever you do and your plans will succeed." Proverbs 16:3

_____

_____

_____

_____

_____

_____

_____

_____

_____

_____

_____

_____

"In the middle of difficulty lies opportunity."
- Albert Einstein

Gratitude/Prayer Journal

Date _____

"Commit to the Lord whatever you do and your plans will succeed." Proverbs 16:3

_____

_____

_____

_____

_____

_____

_____

_____

_____

_____

_____

"Shoot for the moon, even if you miss it, you'll land among the stars!"
- Les Brown

Gratitude/Prayer Journal

Date _____

"Commit to the Lord whatever you do and your plans will succeed." Proverbs 16:3

_____

_____

_____

_____

_____

_____

_____

_____

_____

_____

_____

"The best way out is always through!"
- Robert Frost

Gratitude/Prayer Journal

Date _____

"Commit to the Lord whatever you do and your plans will succeed." Proverbs 16:3

_____

_____

_____

_____

_____

_____

_____

_____

_____

_____

"If you love what you do, you do it well!"
- Malcolm Forbes

Notes/Meditations/Reminders

Gratitude/Prayer Journal

Date _____

"Many are the plans in a man's heart, but it is the Lord's purpose that prevails." Proverbs 19:21

_____
_____
_____
_____
_____
_____
_____
_____
_____
_____

"You get everything in life you want, if you help enough other people get what they want." - Zig Ziglar

Gratitude/Prayer Journal

Date _____

"Many are the plans in a man's heart, but it is the Lord's purpose that prevails." Proverbs 19:21

_____
_____
_____
_____
_____
_____
_____
_____
_____
_____
_____

"What lies behind us and what lies before us are tiny matters compared to what lies within us." - Walt Emerson

Gratitude/Prayer Journal

Date _____

"Many are the plans in a man's heart, but it is the Lord's purpose that prevails." Proverbs 19:21

_____

_____

_____

_____

_____

_____

_____

_____

_____

_____

"Never look at what you have lost… look at what you have left."
- Robert H. Schuller

Gratitude/Prayer Journal

Date _____

"Many are the plans in a man's heart, but it is the Lord's purpose that prevails." Proverbs 19:21

_____

_____

_____

_____

_____

_____

_____

_____

_____

_____

"A passion to do whatever you do in a passionate way. Then you do it well!" - Oscar de la Renta

Gratitude/Prayer Journal

Date _____

"Many are the plans in a man's heart, but it is the Lord's purpose that prevails." Proverbs 19:21

_____

_____

_____

_____

_____

_____

_____

_____

_____

_____

"The successful person is always a learner."
- Norman V. Peale

Gratitude/Prayer Journal

Date _____

"Many are the plans in a man's heart, but it is the Lord's purpose that prevails." Proverbs 19:21

_____

_____

_____

_____

_____

_____

_____

_____

_____

_____

_____

"If you can't change your fate, change your attitude!"
- Amy Tan

Gratitude/Prayer Journal

Date _____

"Many are the plans in a man's heart, but it is the Lord's purpose that prevails." Proverbs 19:21

_____
_____
_____
_____
_____
_____
_____
_____
_____
_____

"No one can put you down without your permission."
- Eleanor Roosevelt

Gratitude/Prayer Journal

Date _____

"Many are the plans in a man's heart, but it is the Lord's purpose that prevails." Proverbs 19:21

"Believe, understand, love and invest in yourself. The B.U.L.I. Process"
- Sara Freeman Smith

Gratitude/Prayer Journal

Date _____

"Many are the plans in a man's heart, but it is the Lord's purpose that prevails." Proverbs 19:21

_____

_____

_____

_____

_____

_____

_____

_____

_____

"God can't fix it until you face it!" - Anonymous

Gratitude/Prayer Journal

Date _____

"Many are the plans in a man's heart, but it is the Lord's purpose that prevails." Proverbs 19:21

_____

_____

_____

_____

_____

_____

_____

_____

_____

_____

"Begin to see it, believe it, and you'll become it!"
- Sara Freeman Smith

Notes/Meditations/Reminders

Gratitude/Prayer Journal

Date _____

"You need to persevere so that when you have done the will of God, you will receive what He has promised." Hebrews 10:36

_____

_____

_____

_____

_____

_____

_____

_____

_____

_____

_____

*"**The tragedy of life is not reaching your goal. It's having no goal to reach!**"* - Dr. Benjamin E. Mays

Gratitude/Prayer Journal

Date _____

"You need to persevere so that when you have done the will of God, you will receive what He has promised." Hebrews 10:36

_____

_____

_____

_____

_____

_____

_____

_____

_____

"A man who says it cannot be done should not interrupt the man doing it!" - Chinese Proverb

Gratitude/Prayer Journal

Date _____

"You need to persevere so that when you have done the will of God, you will receive what He has promised." Hebrews 10:36

_____

_____

_____

_____

_____

_____

_____

_____

_____

_____

_____

"Each of us is created to do something special with our lives."
- Dennis Kimbro

Gratitude/Prayer Journal

Date _____

"You need to persevere so that when you have done the will of God, you will receive what He has promised." Hebrews 10:36

_____
_____
_____
_____
_____
_____
_____
_____
_____
_____
_____

"If you don't know where you're going, any road will take you there."
- Old Proverb

Gratitude/Prayer Journal

Date _____

"You need to persevere so that when you have done the will of God, you will receive what He has promised." Hebrews 10:36

_____
_____
_____
_____
_____
_____
_____
_____
_____
_____
_____
_____

*"**You were born to win. Start thinking, speaking, and acting like a winner.**"* - Susan L. Taylor

Gratitude/Prayer Journal

Date _____

"You need to persevere so that when you have done the will of God, you will receive what He has promised." Hebrews 10:36

_____

_____

_____

_____

_____

_____

_____

_____

_____

"Things start going down when you stop looking up."
- Sara Freeman Smith

Gratitude/Prayer Journal

Date _____

"You need to persevere so that when you have done the will of God, you will receive what He has promised." Hebrews 10:36

"I don't know the key to success, but the key to failure is trying to please everybody." - Bill Cosby

Notes/Meditations/Reminders

"Fear of becoming a has-been keeps some people from becoming anything!"
Deschouieres

Suggested Reading

Purchase a good Study Bible – this is a great way to learn more detail about the history, characters and relationships for each book in the Bible.

My favorite:
Living Insight Study Bible by Charles Swindoll*
*(My Daily Prayer has some excerpts taken from Living Insight Study Bible)

Devotional/Inspirational books:
Experiencing God by Henry T. Blackaby & Claude V. King
Time to Get Serious by Tony Evans
How to Listen to God by Charles Stanley
What Happens When Women Pray by Evelyn Christenson
Simple Abundance Journal of Gratitude by Sarah Ban Breathnach

Personal & Career Development book:
Who Moved My Cheese? An Amazing Way to Deal with Change in Your Work & Life by Dr. Spencer Johnson

> *"Things start going down
> when you stop looking up."*
> *Sara Freeman Smith*

About the Author

Sara can inform while at the same time motivate. She has been speaking since 1989 on a variety of motivational topics to diverse audiences. She has extensive experience speaking in corporations, non-profits, churches, retreats and conferences across the country. During her 30-year executive-management experience, she has assisted and placed thousands of individuals in various employment positions within small to Fortune 500 size companies.

As Founder and President of U R Gems, Inc., Houston, Texas, their primary focus provides motivational and career development training, publishing and speaking. Sara resides in Houston, Texas with her husband, Mack.

Sara Freeman-Smith is available for workshops and speaking engagements. Contact U R Gems Group at info@urgems.com to secure a dynamic speaker, conference presenter, workshop facilitor, or trainer for your next event. You will truly be blessed beyond measure.

> *"Each of us is created to do something special with our lives."*
>
> **Dennis Kimbro**

Other Books by the Author

Turning Stones Into Gems: An Inspirational Self-Development System (First Edition) by Sara Freeman Smith.

Turning Stones Into Gems: An Inspirational Self-Development System (Second Edition) by Sara Freeman Smith.

How to Self-Publish & Market Your Own Book by Mack E. Smith & Sara Freeman Smith (Third Edition). Look for the revised edition which will include social media coming 2024!

Turning Stones Into Gems (The Sequel): Understanding Your Purpose and Maintaining Your Peace Through Life's Challenges. Release date coming in 2024.

> *"There are acres of gems inside each of us!*
>
> *You are a Gem!"*